JOURNEYS

ESSENTIAL TRANSLATIONS SERIES 44

**Canada Council
for the Arts**   **Conseil des Arts
du Canada**

**ONTARIO ARTS COUNCIL
CONSEIL DES ARTS DE L'ONTARIO**

an Ontario government agency
un organisme du gouvernement de l'Ont

Canada

Guernica Editions Inc. acknowledges the support of the Canada Council
for the Arts and the Ontario Arts Council. The Ontario Arts Council
is an agency of the Government of Ontario.

We acknowledge the financial support of the Government of Canada.

JOURNEYS

Nadine Ltaif
Translated by Christine Tipper

GUERNICA
EDITIONS

TORONTO – BUFFALO – LANCASTER (U.K.)
2020

Selections from: *Le livre des dunes* (1999), *Le rire de l'eau* (2004),
Ce que vous ne lirez pas (2010), *Hamra comme par hasard* (2014)

Michael Mirolla, editor
Cover and interior design: Errol F. Richardson
Guernica Editions Inc.
287 Templemead Drive, Hamilton (ON), Canada L8W 2W4
2250 Military Road, Tonawanda, N.Y. 14150-6000 U.S.A.
www.guernicaeditions.com

Distributors:
Independent Publishers Group (IPG)
600 North Pulaski Road, Chicago IL 60624
University of Toronto Press Distribution,
5201 Dufferin Street, Toronto (ON), Canada M3H 5T8
Gazelle Book Services, White Cross Mills
High Town, Lancaster LA1 4XS U.K.

First edition.
Printed in Canada.

Legal Deposit—First Quarter
Library of Congress Catalog Card Number: 2019946619
Title: Journeys / Nadine Ltaif ; translated by Christine Tipper.
Other titles: Poems. Selections. English
Names: Ltaif, Nadine, 1961- author. | Tipper, Christine, translator.
Series: Essential translations series ; 44.
Description: Series statement: Essential translations series ; 44 | Poems translated from Le livre des dunes, Le rire de l'eau, Ce que vous ne lirez pas, and Hamra comme par hasard.
Identifiers: Canadiana 20190155078 | ISBN 9781771834070 (softcover)
Classification: LCC PS8573.T34 A2 2020 | DDC C841/.54—dc23

CONTENTS

IN THE BOSOM OF NOUN*

Here I am plunged into the centre of the earth
curled around myself like an earthworm.
I unravel subterranean words
that destroy me.
I plunge into the maze
like a shell isolated from everything.
No one will uncover my story from beneath.
I will not give myself up.
Such resistance deserves being burnt at the stake.
I've been plunged into hell for three months and more.
I am numerous, multiple.
Too much love is lost.
Each house move means I must start again.
Each morning I meet the rootlessness that speaks to me.
I watch naked trees and I strip off my self.

No, Noun you have done nothing.
The effort of building knocks me down.
Nature triumphs once again.
I am not alone in building the universe.
Creation continues without me.
Wisdom eludes me.
I am abandoned.
I play at love despite myself.
Love remains alone
in the shadows, in the night
the day takes it, takes me
I disappeared from the sky.

You will stay in hell
you will not germinate
in the subterranean depths of memories
faced with the crime you dare not commit.
Will you shatter those things that slowly wear you down?
Will you extract what is eating at you?
Will I get rid of myself one day?
No one sees what is hidden
in a river of love.
A torrent of passion
opens rock, splits me in two.
To be two at least, to be three, to be four.
My love does not see
when an awful and dislocated dance
throws me outside of myself.
My words make no sense
because I am alone in loving like this
accumulating dreams
enduring realities.
The earth is pulled from under my feet.

My feet are not stable.
I do not have a good head on my shoulders.
I do not have a right hand that writes.
I do not have a body free to be itself.
No one to judge me
and yet I remain there
too weak to disappear completely
from the horizon.

The day dawns
the sky will not turn any colour.
I passed a night of absence.
I didn't reign in the sky, or on the earth.
I didn't smile my Oriental smile.
I didn't take on the curves of love.
I continued to diminish.
I persist in losing weight
nothing can stop me.

I start from the beginning again.
I grow a few feathers
like a fledgling
fallen from its nest.
I am in constant movement.
Not a single root grows.
Not a single memory has come to shatter my exile.
My back always rounded
under the burden of solitude.
My solitude, no one sees it
because I do not want to see anyone.
My passion is too scary for
anyone who perceives it.
I am always hunched over
under a Sky that wants nothing to do with me.
In the Bosom of Noun
the Earth in its sorrow
not a single root grows.

Now the exodus chant
like an ascent towards a hell of seven skies.
I knock on seven doors. The eighth will open for me.
I am at the eighth door. Have I finally got rid of myself?
Have I taken off seven skins, unravelled seven languages?
Did I go and place a kiss on seven lips?
When my hand will have liberated
the thousands of blacks chained by very pure hands
the seventh day, I will then be able to rest.
But nothing is finished and I have begun nothing
I arrived there, by chance and by what pure chance.
I found myself with my feet planted.
Will I descend into the earth like a fatality?
Traverse darkness like Hecate with a thousand torches?
Will I mature? Love within me is happy and makes me anew.
I refuse to begin again. I refuse to give of myself.
I am a bee attracted by the Orchid.
I am a woman pursued by a warrior.
And I pick the poison from a beach at Sour**.

* Noun: in Egyptian mythology, a primordial ocean where all things are born.
** Lebanese village that used to be called Tyre.
Extract from *Le livre des dunes*, Nadine Ltaif, Editions du Noroît, Montréal, 1999

SCENES FROM CARTHAGE

This morning I plunged
into the arms of death.
I immersed myself in wisdom.

In the silence
the secret
the mystery
of Carthage.

The roots of a palm tree bury a Tophet.

*

In the shadow of a palm grove
lay the tombs of dead children

A female cat, in a hieratic pose
at the far end of the site
stares fixedly at me.
The Punic palm trees
are rigidly penitent.

In the movement of the ground
the stones do battle
with the roots.

Both: conquerors and conquered are intertwined.

*

Fig trees, date palms, or immense jerids
are prostrated towards the ground.

The most ancient site of
Phoenician conquests welcomes one of their
survivors.

They bequeath to others
their vain battles.

*

Young infant boys
in their thousands
have received a stele in their memory.

The girls do not measure up;
they do not appease the cannibal sources.

When the town was in danger
cruel kings
weighed upon its conscience
the weight of an elephant.

*

The sign of the goddess-mother
Tanit haloed by a lunar crescent
watches over its grief.

The same female cat
a real ancestor
appears at the other end of the site.

This time she smiles at me.

When I lifted my head
she had disappeared.

HAGAR

For Hejer

Beginning of May
I carry
the cruelty of births
more painfully than the fall
of leaves in autumn.

I live the desert
even though the month of May has begun.
I keep within me a desert
a winter from which I do not heal.

I only have the word love
to quench my thirst
my body for a boat
and no one with whom to navigate.
I traverse the silence like a sea of dunes.
I keep the trace of your footprints for words.

I am no longer capable of suffering, Hagar
I'm no longer afraid of myself.
My desire becomes a desire without hunger.

And you, desert of absence
in your emptiness
I live absence.

It is difficult for me to be an Arab

or to carry an image in my name.

It is difficult to be proud
or to love
or to cease to love.

No sign no grain of sand
signals your presence.

Teach me to breathe Hagar
your dune perfume
on my body half-dead in the other
who is no longer there.
In the inertia and cowardice of existence.

The desert possesses me
I am born of the desert.
My body made of sand and words.

I would not know how to capture you
on my cheek
your caress is like
the sting of a slap
when I attempt to hold back the wind.

You do not know
you my erg my desert
when a being inspires you
it erupts in you.

A muse inspires you
and you are transformed.
The foundations are shaken.

My body opens
a new me emerges
from a burning lava.

An earthquake
anger mounts
the vital sap of destruction.

Black hair
an intense mouth
a Tuareg sculpts my skin
moved, to want to capture
an instant her portrait.

Her eyes are so black
she floors me
such is her beauty.

Nude, an open look, transparent
To wild love, entranced, vibrant
on the route of the senses.

I no longer manage to distinguish
cries of ecstasy from cries of suffering.

ANDALUSIAN EXILE

Spain, November 2006

ANDALUSIAN EXILE

In this same park
corner of Ontario and Saint Urbain.
Another engulfed town
discovered during recent digs
and it's an explosion in my head
that exults at this discovery.

Nothing leaves its mark.
Tarsus. Completely engulfed?
Only fragments of writing
recount the commerce
between Tyre and King Hiram
Tyre from where gold came
Tarsus, ancient Seville
range of civilisations.

BETWEEN RELICS AND DISAPPEARANCES

I stand there.
Wars wipe out
populations and towns
if not cataclysms.
And we are
on the other side
of the small screen.

GIRALDA

You have to climb very high
to see from the summit
the extent of the horror.

Hatred and pride
are twin sisters
that bring down each other.
I am
an ache with no name.

Who had wanted to dig up
the body to crucify it
one more time
to spread out their victory
on a hill
for all to see.

Who had just poked out
the eyes of his enemy
to install his reign
wiping out the seeds
of a people and violating
their descendants.

GUERNICA

All the streets
where we walked
yesterday: Fuencaral Atocha
Anton Martin
near to where we are staying
had been bombed.
In Queen Sophia's museum
the metamorphosis of the painting
of Guernica.
There where the violence of
Spain
spread before us
in its ultimate cruelty.
Streets in the capital's
Metros
full of refugees.

A horse
mouth screaming
crushes a body
with eyes bulging
under its hoof.

The Minotaur
now a symbol
of Spain
repeats the toreador's
cry.

The mother holding
her dead child
like a pieta,
a look still focussed
on a bloody past.

Black and white
Guernica's war.
Grey colour lit
by a candle
or a lamp
like an ocular sun
always open.

SEVILLE (GIRALDA 2)

A tower
A step
An ascent
I follow it
Thirty floors
A slope
No steps
Where the horse and muezzin
passed
five times
to call his prayers
A tower
and its walls
that separate cultures
between the sumptuous
cathedral
overwhelmingly, crushingly
Catholic
and the uncluttered tower
written in Arabic
in Old Seville
in the Vera Cruz
certain crimes
can remain
unpunished
I remain transfixed
in the fear
of a nightmare.
I'm there.

Weary from the passing years
the centuries
like two refugees
from a Goya painting
or in exile
Jew or Muslim
We are chased away
Her mother will take
with her
oranges from Seville
jasmine from Seville
roses from Seville
and the Spanish cuisine
that will only exist
in the North
of Tunisia
She will continue
to cook
the dishes of Seville
or of Cordoba
I don't know
why
there had to be so much
suffering
and the ascent
of the tower
is an atonement
a purification
the weariness of centuries

twenty-one minus
seven
I've never known how to count
it could be
fourteen
centuries
that separate us
from the suffering
and the vengeance
continues to decimate
the tribal chiefs
the political assassination
I cannot
believe that
it can
endure
The mosaic
that completes
the portrait
the puzzle
of history
that we try
to extract from
the circle of hell
by climbing
this tower
like a pilgrimage
to Mecca.

But she
she already seems
to have walked
in the streets
of Seville
to have entered the fray
with the flamenco dance
to have danced to the rhythms
of the flamenco
to the beat
of feet
of hands
of feet that crush
under their sabots
like the hardness
of stones and rocks
to the sound of a guitar
streaming
with sweat
or blood
like a bull
in the ring
under the lances
of the toreador
its sharpened horns
continue
to charge at his adversary
his enemy
in love

like water
but it's the pain
of the flamenco song
of lovemaking
the cries are from Spain
that weeps over its history
of love and blood.

SANTA JUSTA

No justice
will be had
whilst the blood
of vengeance
flows
whilst the blood
calls to blood
calls to blood
calls to blood
blood that flows
over the centuries
of blood
Santa Justa
Saint Justice,
becomes Saint
and just
like the hand
of a clock
at the depart
of a train.

The train leaves
Seville held by the centuries
of unquenched vengeance.
The return to the past
has finished in the present.
The present will be a series
of small violent acts
and enormous pain.

The moments of peace
found in the garden
of jasmines
of cypress
of bougainvillea
These moments of fusion
where art succeeds
in vanquishing the racial
hatred
where the great of Toledo
and those of Arabia
When the Jews and Muslims
and Christians
embellish their efforts
They find a song
a stone
a new tale
to sculpt with
love
They raise Alcazar
where the *mujer* room
Like the passion
of a meeting
that traverses
hatred
traverses time.

LIKE SAINT SEBASTIAN

Martyr
I was on a horse
I fought the Moors
The horse still alive
My breastplate pierced
by a lance
Pegasus carries me
in the beyond
It's a plane
that carries me
towards the New World.

NINE GIRLS WILL BE AS STRONG AS AN ELEPHANT

India, 16 January 2006

NINE GIRLS WILL BE AS STRONG
AS AN ELEPHANT

for Yolande Villemaire

It's like going back in time
to our previous lives.
It's a return to the sources of Islam.
To the towns of Northern India
to the cradle of a thousand and one nights.
A journey in the space of time
that leads to the India of a thousand doors
of multiple animal voices.
Sometimes without voice sometimes
Sappho the philosopher
sometimes a Temple dancer
Ishtar the sacred prostitute
or Greek Caryatids.
A companion follows me
I meet her in various places.
Sometimes mother
sometimes sister
a genuine love binds us.
I grow up surrounded by pain
and I escape towards the West.
I meet a Frenchman,
then a Québécois.
Depending on the century.
He is a Crusader.
He's going to fight in the Middle Ages.
He would have been an Englishman in India.
Everything needs deciphering

reality is an enigma.
I search for the meanings of fate
Who are these beings that hold out their hand
to you?
Who are these others who set a trap
for you?
I pass through these landscapes
flora and fauna read about in a thousand and one nights.
A peacock jumps from one tree to another, a sign of roy-
alty.
He screeches like a little girl being raped.
Indian jasmine.
Poppies from the North.
Cruelty and gentleness,
wars and peace follow one another
at great speed
the watch hand
rewinds time
an accelerated film
in reverse
I advance
planted in the decor of a thousand and one nights
I see India's influence
on Islamic civilisation
the largest mosque in Asia
Jamia Masjid.
Yamouna hadn't wanted to be chosen
by the Maharaja to be a part of his harem.
She sticks close to Radika and her other sisters.

The nine of them will be as strong as an elephant
to fight against this injustice.

Reclusive, forbidden, left to wait upon their king,
they live, breathe, cannot celebrate
before the arrival of this ignoble husband
who amuses himself by making sometimes one,
sometimes another, jealous.

In their golden cages,
they live in exile.

Separated, imported
from another kingdom,
the kingdom of their birth
they serve as a blood link
to ratify the chain of solidarity
with enemy kingdoms.

A XII century Indian,
Rajpoute.
He had twelve wives,
twelve Maharani
and I was one of them.

Isolated in my room,
I waited for his visits
every evening.

Centuries have passed,
sometimes he is my brother-in-arms,
sometimes my sister,
sometimes my mother.
Hungry for the things of love.

Behind closed doors,
doors incrusted with ivory
sealed with a large padlock
that shuts in the wives
keeping them for their one and only master.
She sings
like a canary
behind her closed door.
She lets out the sigh
of a slave,
not free.
She recites her pain
in her poems
that she writes with her tears.

FROM JAIPUR

The sensation of having been here before lingers within me.
To have lived this suffering.
The suffering of rocks eroded
by the centuries.
The rocks of the XII century.
Palaces of the Maharajah,
where the first stories were told
about Scheherazade.

A princess suffered
between these skeletal walls,
that seem fossilized,
like a conch
eaten by time.

IN A PHOTO

A young, very young
bride,
enveloped in an orange sari,
her face covered with a veil,
of transparent muslin,
she is accompanied by her mother
who seems to be my age.

She is at the entrance of a *Haveli*
part of an ancient bourgeois home
now an hotel.
She remains immobile.
She seems to want
to say something to us.
We find it hard
to understand her message.

Fortunately,
Yolande is there,
she half understands:
"She said that she wants to show us her face".

I'm surprised
how to understand
this offering
this desire to unveil
for us who are from
the West.

She raises
the light veil
feverishly.
And then:
we are stunned
by the beauty
of her face.
A chiselled jewel in her nose.
She smiles.
Her hands are decorated with henna
they are of ancient sculptures,
her brown skin
and fruity perfume.
I remain transfixed
my camera in my pocket
incapable of seizing this timeless
moment,
rooted in the millennium space of an India
contemporary and profound.
She has given us the gift
of her face
this forbidden fruit.
She has shared it
when she should have kept it for her husband
Why?

I attempt to pierce the mystery of India
and India's secret remains sealed.

No other country has left me with this impression of depth
and of mystery.
Perhaps she wanted us to transport her image with us
to the West
so that she can exult in a perfume of freedom
for she knows that elsewhere
freedom exists
for her as well.
I try to understand again
my unease when confronted
with this gift of a face
from a young bride
all in orange
veiled.

THE ROOM

The room walls are so high!
four or five metres in height.
those sort of heights are not found in Quebec
or elsewhere
I have never seen any so high.
In these cages where princesses
were shut away locked up
it was necessary to create
an illusion of liberty
perhaps it was
for this reason that the walls
were so high.
Even in the most luxurious of places
I could not describe
the impression, the dread I felt
at the sight of that heavy padlock
that had to be sealed
when leaving the bedroom
in the hotel
feelings of terrifying
fear.

HAMRA

PHOINIKE

Because of the copper
colour of their skin

The Greeks called them
The 'Reds' – the 'Phoenicians'

Sea travellers
covered by the colour
of sun
on their shoulders

Open faced
ardent smiles

Hot blood
tender heart
easy tears.

BEIRUT-THE-RED

Cadmosian
phoinikian
of murex
antique shell
a purple colour
that was the glory
of a whole people.

BEIRUT-HAMRA

To Hejer, Faten, Yolande

With three friends we have come on a pilgrimage
to the land of our Phoenician ancestors. Here we are
gathered in a small hotel in the heart of Beirut.

The birds chirp loudly in the sky this Sunday morning.
Cars sleep in my childhood neighbourhood.
I was thirteen.

Images from my distant past explode in my head.
The oldest houses have remained the most beautiful.

From the balcony of our hotel, I contemplate a house
covered by a Roman roof, healed from its war scars.

Palms, giant eucalyptus, fig mingle
with jasmine and olive trees.

The pollution and noise have taken the day off in Beirut
on this Sunday morning.

Everything comes back to me, the street names
the polluted odour
mixed with humidity

With all the changes that it has undergone
I recognise the city
in its excitement, in its madness

Beirut enjoying its
morning

      Beirut with its gentle
wind caressing
the foliage

      On the window of
the building opposite
a plane's image
passes over every
five minutes.

Choices are not fortuitous
And chance does not exist
      We have chosen
to stay in Hotel Elissa.
      The least renovated
in Beirut-Hamra

Beirut-the-Red

The furniture, chairs,
      sofas, tables and lace
doilies in plastic
      from the 1970s

Since the war
      since I left
Beirut in 1975.

RUE HAMRA'S NEWSPAPER KIOSK

I make my way towards the newspaper kiosk to buy *L'Orient-Le Jour*. The old man is dozing. I wake him up. I find *L'Express* with an article on the Salafi movement in Tunisia, not *L'Orient-Le Jour*. "It's out of stock", the man with tired eyes worn out from reading tells me. Never mind, I need some change, I hand him my 50,000 pound note. He raises his eyes: You want *L'Orient?* Yes, please. He leaves his kiosk, waddles across the small rue Hamra, confident, towards the Librairie d'Orient. He's absent for a while. Then he waddles back to his kiosk slaloming through the cars as he'd always done and enters his little newspaper trailer. Triumphant, he hands me the newspaper.

YES, BEIRUT HAS CHANGED

Relics wave
to me

        I remember a name
the shapes of shops
or hotels
The Paradise
the Wardiyé petrol station
the Capuchins
where I took my first
communion even if
I am not a
Catholic.

Domptex,
the Way Inn bookshop
the fresh juice merchant:
The Maison Rouge
An orange juice
sweetened

New places have been added
With F. we discover
the intellectuals' café, the Ta Marbouta
And every morning
breakfast
at Kaakaya's

Traditional music
goes to our heads
like the chicha that accompanies
an evening of Euro football.

ELISSA HOTEL

We have chosen
a non-renovated hotel
that has remained as it was
before the civil war

The receptionist
veiled
wearing heavy make-up
is our host

Her family runs the place
I feel no sense of rejection
        faced with her veil
that resembles an adornment

Welcoming
in perfect English.

Every morning
I wake up
a song of
Fayrouz in my head

The small hill
of Beirut-the-Red
pulls me along in its turbulence
of traffic jams and horns

Everything must go fast
like commercial
transactions

We walk quickly
in Beirut

All the better
It keeps us fit
with a zest for life.

KAAKAYA

Every morning, we meet for the Arabian breakfast. Lebanese, labneh or foul! The waiter is happy to see us arrive, one after the other, in rhythm with our waking. Beautiful smile. I will learn later that he is Syrian. He asks us our names. For how long will we display our identities at each new encounter? I tell him mine. My paternal grandmother came from Homs. And your other grandparents? He mentions the L.s from Rachaya. Ah, yes, that's the maternal branch of my family tree. This tree with its weighty fruit is so heavy! And my paternal grandfather from Zahle, in the Bekaa valley. But yes, there are L.s who left for Brazil! Oh! of course, my grandfather's brothers. That's it, I've been caught! He will be able to place me. He has recognised where I come from, and now I've been admitted into the clan! When will we escape from this clannish mentality! I think of my Quebecois in-laws. They received me at their table, fed me without asking me about my origins, or my identity. There you are. I've been served up as a good breakfast.

THE OLD LADY AND THE ROSES

It is almost midnight
She decides to go out
to work at this late
hour
When clients
a little drunk
perhaps
will buy roses from her

An old lady
hunchbacked
walks through the café
a bouquet of roses
red and white
in her arms

What is your name madam?
How stupid of me to ask her
such a question.
She won't answer it.
H. buys a rose from her
She gives her two more
she moves on
leaves the café.

1975

Fateful date
of separations
of ruptures
The roads cut off
          No longer possible to pass
from East to West
without risking one's life
We circulated
          freely
from South to North
from North to South
          imprisoned
in our respective regions.

F. had not gone
up in to the regions
of Mount Lebanon

N. had never gone down
to the villages in the South

F. would discover the deep
valleys

N. the diversity of
the orchards

Forbidden to enter during
the nineteen years of
religious conflicts

They unite
now
their differences.

YA BAYÉ YA BAYÉ YA BAYÉ!

I stop a random taxi. A Ford from the seventies. The old toothless driver is a relic. Obviously, those years won't let go of my memory. Take me to Broummana, please. By the new road. Do you know the new road? He doesn't answer. He drives from West Beirut towards Achrafier, turns right. In fact, he seems not to know it. Traffic jam. I say: as if you were going to Jbeil. There's a new motorway. He says: Oh, but I should never have come this way! *Ya bayé ya bayé ya bayé!* No, it would have been best to take the road from the new town centre. *Ya bayé ya bayé!* He corrects his route. He drives. Go past the big tree. It's my mother's reference point. Do you mean the Kataeb's office? If you wish. He drives. He stops, fills up with petrol. He didn't think he would be doing such a long twenty-minute drive, used to driving only in Hamra – a block of houses. Drive until McDo and then turn right at the Joura-Broummana sign. Finally, he discovers the great big motorway. The old man transforms into James Bond. He puffs out his chest and pushes down on the accelerator. No traffic jam, he is happy. Climbing the hills, the bends are sharper and steeper. He re-joins the old road, the streets become narrow. Dreading, at each bend, a car coming the other way. The place where my parents live is nicely tucked away, the old Ford has to go down in to the valley again. *Ya bayé ya bayé!* When I pay my fare, he offers me his toothless smile. My name is Riyad. Thank you Riyad. Have a good return trip. Will you be able to find your way back? You can take the old road if you want. By going towards the main road.

HOTEL HIT

We are staying
as if by chance
at less than three hundred metres
from the place of my childhood

The place we were expulsed from

The hotel built by my father
still stands

in a tiny little street
behind the B. Pharmacy

the haven of happiness
that exploded in my head
in 1975

obliging us to flee
to give our building
to refugees from
camps in the South

'Pack your cases,
we are leaving', says my father

And without taking anything with us
we left Lebanon.
The young man at reception
almost chokes
on hearing my name

Will we know one day
whether chance meets
destiny
People encountered
during our childhood
meeting
on the corner of a street
will they recognise each other?

At the end of the tiny little street
the B. Pharmacy
the meeting point
for school children

Where does one story start?
Where does it finish?

In the same episode
that started it.

Someone rings the bell
I open wide
with a big 'hello'

The young man freezes
I don't notice the weapon
the Kalashnikov behind his back

He replies to my greeting
I see his youth again

He won't hurt me

My child-minder
opens the door a little
opposite

Suspicious
'There are nine of us
in this house
there isn't
room for you
to stay'.

Hundreds of them arrive
young people armed
with their families

     At the hotel reception
they ask for my brothers

     'We are looking for
two fighters
named S. and C.'
My father stunned
begs them
to leave.
'You've made a mistake
there is no one called S. or C.
my sons aren't
fighters.'

What courage father!
With a weapon
pointing at you
What composure!
He attempts to make them laugh
puts on an Egyptian accent
Turns the tragedy
into comedy
and manages
to make the refugees
withdraw.

Many years later
Twenty years and more

We move to
the mountains
A friend of my mother
At the end of an evening
and quite unexpectedly
talking about the past
tells us
that she was the mother of two fighters
named S. and C.

We then found out that C. was the elder and S.
the younger.

THIS YOU WILL NOT READ

THIS YOU WILL NOT READ

For Monique Bosco

I write a letter that you will not read. This time I'm sure. You will not read it. Unless you are an angel that continues to dictate your words sitting on my shoulder, like a piece of Bach music that travels through time and returns swelling, insistent and says: continue, continue, don't stop, please don't, write like you've never written before, with delectation. Love, like writing, like life, every day, rubs shoulders with death. This proximity, you have never felt it before.

It remains to finish the book. To turn the page and close it. To open another.

Now, I feel diminished before her splendid absence. The luminous rays of her smile. And all of an inheritance with which I know not what to do. I need to rediscover the scent of the Lebanese mountains pines. And I find myself in no man's land. Alone with my pen that tries to row.

I know, we are always starting again, like a day that dawns and a day that turns to night.

We emerge from the night, when the night seems an endless tunnel. And we are surprised to still be alive. All of this has been just a dream, so hard to swallow. Dream or reality. Everything is reality. Even a dream. Especially a dream. Certain people are nourished by dreams, as if a freedom. To break the frontier between dream and reality. What courage to penetrate the dream zones. But it takes a greater courage to penetrate reality. A zone from which we are not sure to leave alive. Breathless. Flayed alive from what we see parade before us: wars, atrocities, injustices, the book of a history that does not end.

My inheritance is to continue to slide my pen across the page, to trace a groove across the sea. A trace that will disappear like a body that disintegrates.

I see birds come to land on the electric wire of a music that joins that of the waters of the New Brunswick Sea. Waters that speak of the slow but necessary metamorphosis of separation from river to sea.

The separation of the sea and river happens gently, without limits, without frontiers. Fish from freshwaters do not mix with fish from salt waters.

Each species remains in its waters. Only we, humans, have the capacity to live in both waters.
Freshwaters, salt waters. Bittersweet writing.

Everything concurs to create the music. The wind in the trees, the symphony of spirited leaves. Rustling or silence. All is music, all is words of silence in seas of absence.

I'm at a turning point. And what is waiting for me at the corner of the street, is a surprise. I don't know. I don't apprehend it. But I've lost all my naivety. Reality has become my primary state. Even if my capacity for fantasizing is great. It stretches as far as the fine sand dunes of Miscou Island.

I WALK IN OUTREMONT

I walk in Outremont
I look at a peony
She loved peonies
She loved anemones
She loved poppies
I mixed them up them

A death
that accompanies you
that walks with you

If I look at a fern
I remember the ferns
that we came across
during our walks
on Mount Royal.

And she walks with me

HAVE YOU EVER CRUSHED A FLOWER

Have you ever crushed a flower
                in a notebook?
if you have, did you notice
how it leaves an imprint of its heart
                through the pages?
it strips off, leaves its trace
page after page
until all that is left
is a little drop of soul.
In the same way the body
                disappears at the moment
                of death.
The soul rises to heaven
when the breath joins the wind,
the clouds the plants and all
the rest of the living.

YOU HAVE GONE

You have gone
and wars continue
questions remain
and I remain in
your hands.

I searched for
beauty
I found
war

But here is the miracle
I wanted silence
I found
music

I searched for
reason
I found
madness

I searched for peace
I found
passion

And passion reigned

THE CRAVING FOR LIFE

The craving for life
was all that mattered
and not the craving
for death

Today I've understood
that the craving for death
is also
a craving for life

And even if
writing
tasted luxury

it had tasted
poverty

and it had never known how
to detach from it

Writing is a
painting
and is without mercy

Purity and ugliness
mix together
in words
the words that you still dictate to me:

powerful words
powerless words
worries
You would have said

But being Asiatic
as I am
I say:
to write is to paint life
in its ugliness
and its beauty.

To write is to write death
each book is an adieu
and ultimate adieu
each book is a suicide.

If everything is a drawing
in any case
if after all everything
were just writing
a story
a History
the most fascinating
of stories

Between the taste for freedom
and the respect of the law
I discovered the Goose's tale
do you remember?

Today dear lady
you would have celebrated your eightieth birthday
it is 8 in the morning
on the roof a warm wind
prepares a pleasant day
30 degrees is forecast
you would not have liked
this day

THIS BRINGS TO AN END
THE BOOK OF YOUR LIFE

This brings to an end the book of your life
your body decided to finish
its material life
how alone we are going to feel
in our daily routine
what remains of you
your laugh
your presence
your absence
and summer without you
and autumn without you
and winter without you
the most difficult
will be spring
without you.

ABOUT THE AUTHOR

Nadine Ltaif is a Lebanese woman who was born in Cairo in 1961. She has lived in Montreal for most of her adult life. Her first book, *Les Métamorphoses d'Ishtar* was published by Guernica in 1987. Since then Nadine has published a number of poetry collections including:

Entre les fleuves, Montreal, Guernica, 1991. Finalist in the Emile-Nelligan Prize 1991. English translation by Christine Tipper: *Changing Shores*, Toronto, Guernica, 2009.
Elégies du Levant, Montreal, Editions du Noroit, 1995
Le Livre des dunes, Montreal, Editions du Noroit, 1999
Le Rire de l'eau, Montreal, Editions du Noroit, 2005
Ce que vous ne lirez pas, Montreal, Editions du Noroit, 2010
Hamra comme par hasard, Montreal, Editions du Noroit, 2014
Rien de mon errance, Montreal, Editions du Noroit, 2019

Nadine is one of the most original poets of her generation.

ABOUT THE TRANSLATOR

Christine Tipper holds a Ph.D. and a Masters in French literary translation from the University of Exeter, England, and is a Member of the Chartered Institute of Linguists and of the Conseil International d'Études Francophones. She works as a freelance interpreter, translator and a freelance teacher of translating and interpreting on Masters programmes at the University of Bath. She has translated several authors for Guernica including *Changing Shores* by Nadine Ltaif, Evelyne Wilwerth's *Smile, you're getting old*, Danielle Fournier's *We Come From The Same Light* and Francis Catalano's *Where Spaces Glow*.

Printed in September 2019
by Gauvin Press,
Gatineau, Québec